# Set Up Your Own Platform

**How to create and own your website, newsletter, and social media presence**

Andy Sylvester

**Easy Tech Press**
**Wilsonville, Oregon**

Copyright © 2021 Andy Sylvester

First printing 2021

All rights reserved. No part of this book my be reproduced or transmitted in any form or by any means, electronic or mechanical, including photocopying, recording, or by any information storage and retrieval system, without written permission from the author, except for brief quotations in a review.

All trademarks within this guide belong to their legitimate owners.

Published by:
Easy Tech Press
P. O. Box 1018
Wilsonville, Oregon 97070
USA

http://www.easytechpress.com
info@easytechpress.com


ISBN 978-1-7373143-0-1

# Table of Contents

# Introduction

During the summer of 2020, a series of protests took place in Portland, Oregon. As they continued, I started to collect links for my own record. As I read stories, I saw that there were multiple points of view (participants, reporters, news organizations), and I wanted to try to follow their posts. I ended up creating a news app to collect all of these different sources (http://portlandprotests.andysylvester.com/ ). In discussions with Ken Smith, Professor of English at University of Indiana South Bend, Ken offered these comments:

> I seem to recall that you mentioned wanting to push back against the transience of the usual news formats. Stories appear, and then they are replaced by the next day's stories, and the next, and some of these documents become increasingly hard to locate after a few days. In addition, without a collection of diverse voices and the unfolding of stories over time, it's hard to have much confidence in one's understanding or in the conclusions being drawn by any particular participant or news organization. Catching, reviewing and sorting, annotating of sources along the way, commenting on patterns as they unfold--the complexity of the struggles in Portland seemed to require this much, perhaps more.

I decided to create a web site to capture these links I was reading and to provide a level of filtering and analysis. The site (https://portlandprotestnews.com/ ) went live on September 1, 2020. I made a daily post to the site through mid-October 2020, summarizing the best links of the previous day's activity. A hospital visit in late October interrupted my posting, and eventually I decided to discontinue posting to the site. However, the skills I built up and the tools that I built, assembled, and used could be applied to any special-interest/special-topic website. As a final contribution, I am creating a guide to capture how I went about creating this site. It will serve as a record for myself for future efforts, but also will be a toolkit that can be used by anyone as a guide for this type of journalism.

# Chapter 1 – Define Your Goal

This chapter will walk you through a process to define what you want to do with your site.

## Pick A Topic

We all have topics we are interested in, and follow these topics in various ways. There are many news organizations publishing stories on the Web. These can be followed through the use of news feeds/RSS feeds in a feed reader app, or social media like Twitter. People who use Twitter, Facebook, or Instagram follow people or organizations to keep up on what those people or organizations are posting. The nature of those services (feed reader, Twitter, etc.) is that they present a stream or river of posts within their user interface, with the most recent posts at the beginning or top of the user interface, and older posts further down from the recent posts. In all of these posts, though, there are probably one or two or three topics that may be more interesting than others, topics that you focus on first when you scroll through the stream or river of current posts. Pick one of those topics to start your journey on developing a special topic website. And always remember - you can always change your mind later! Whatever skills you pick up along the way can be applied to future endeavors.

## Find Sources

As an exercise, let us assume that you have picked an initial topic and are starting to list potential sources of news and information to follow. This exercise will use the topic of the protests in Portland, Oregon. The first area I focused on was the news organizations in the Portland area. In Portland, the newspaper of record is The Oregonian, so I started with reviewing the site for RSS feeds. I was surprised to find that the current website for the newspaper (https://www.oregonlive.com/ ) has no RSS feeds at all -

amazing! It does, however, have a number of Twitter feeds, and many of the reporters have Twitter accounts.

I then moved on to other newspapers/websites in the Portland area, most of which had RSS feeds, and added those to the list. As I reviewed these sites, I also made note of reporters who had Twitter accounts or separate websites. After that, I reviewed the websites for the TV stations that had local news broadcasts, adding those feeds/Twitter accounts to the list. I then turned to government sources, since there were several areas that had interaction with the protests (Portland police, Portland city council, county law enforcement (county sheriff), county government, state police, and state government). Most of the Portland city council had individual Twitter accounts and used them on a regular basis to get information out on areas of interest to them. This was also the same for the police chief, county sheriff and governor, so I added their accounts to the list. Next, I looked for independent reporters covering the protests. From news accounts in the summer of 2020, I noticed that The Oregonian and a number of local TV stations would link directly to Twitter posts from these reporters. This was a pleasant surprise, as I have seen many media organizations refuse to link to news organizations or sources other than their own. Again, these were added to the list.

Finally, I looked for organizations that were participating in the protests. These included groups like Portland's Resistance, Don't Shoot Portland, and other advocacy groups. Some of these groups only had Facebook accounts, but others had websites with RSS feeds. Most of these groups also had some other social media presence on Twitter or Instagram. Other non-profit organizations such as churches should also be considered.

To summarize, once you have selected a topic, start with looking for mainstream news sources, government organizations, advocacy groups, and independent news sources. If you are focusing on a popular topic (a new video game, TV, or some other activity or event), services like Twitter, Facebook, Snapchat and TikTok may be your primary sources.

4  Find Sources

# Chapter 2 – Gather Information

This chapter will describe tools to collect information for your website.

## Creating a Twitter List

In the previous chapter on collecting sources, one of the prime ways to follow what is happening from a source is through its Twitter feed. Twitter provides a way to group a set of the people you follow on Twitter into lists. The content from a list can then be viewed separately from the content from all of the people you follow on Twitter. Here is a set of steps to set up a Twitter list from a desktop browser.

Click on the Lists link in the navigation bar on the left side of the screen:

Home

Explore

Notifications

Messages

Bookmarks

Lists

Profile

More

Tweet

Click on the "Create New Lists" icon at the top of the window (see icon circled):

A new window will appear:

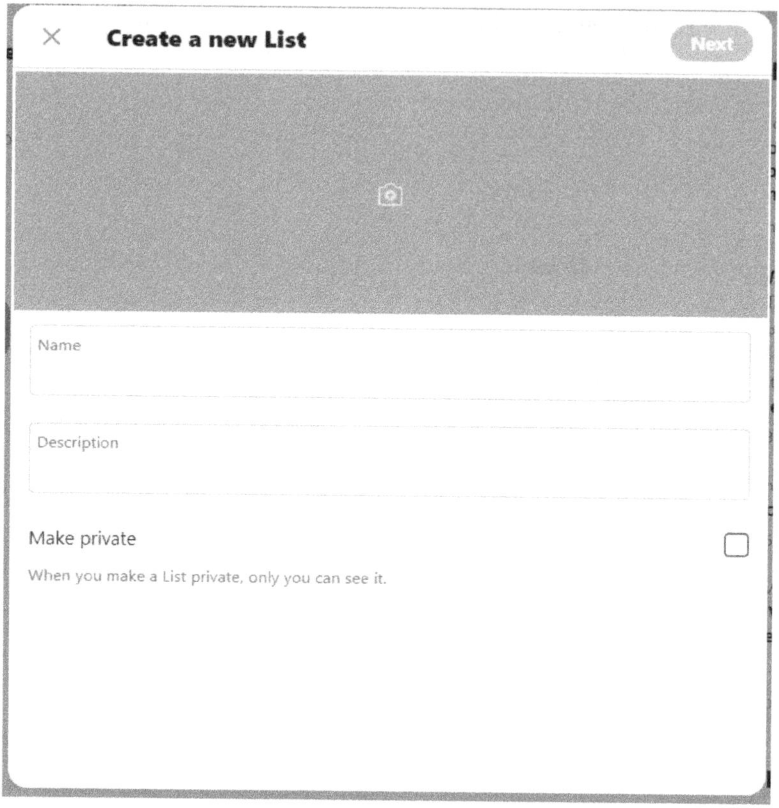

| ✕    **Create a new List**              Next |
| --- |

Name

Description

Make private ☐

When you make a List private, only you can see it.

Enter a name for the list and a short description of the list. List names cannot be longer than 25 characters, and they cannot start with a number. Finally, you can choose to make the list private (only you can see it) or public (any Twitter user could view the curated content from the list). After completing the above steps, click the Next button at the top right corner of the window. A new window will appear:

Click in the search text box to start looking for Twitter users to add to the list. They do not have to be accounts you are currently following. Here is an example:

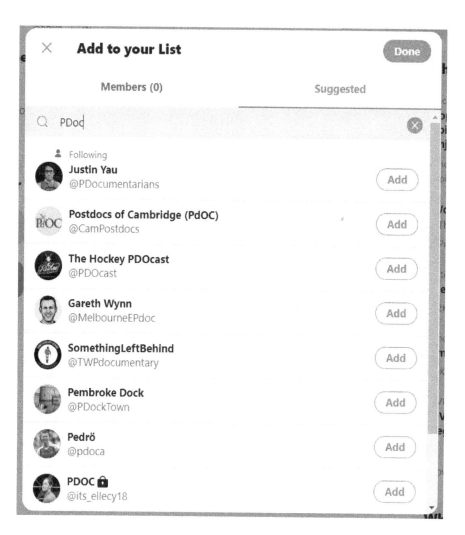

Click on the Add button to add users to the list. When you click on Add, that will be replaced with a "Remove" button.

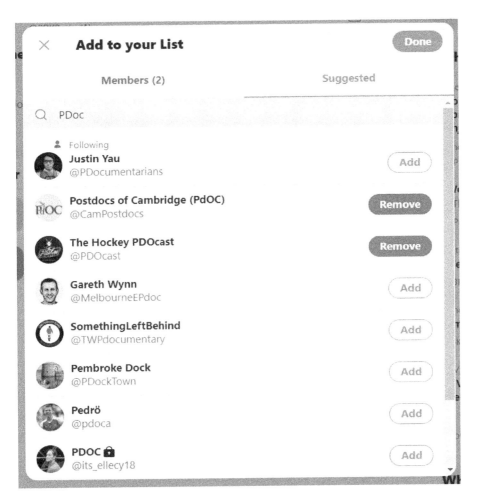

When you are finished adding users to the list, click the Done button in the upper right corner of the window. The main Twitter window will return and start to display content from the users in the new list.

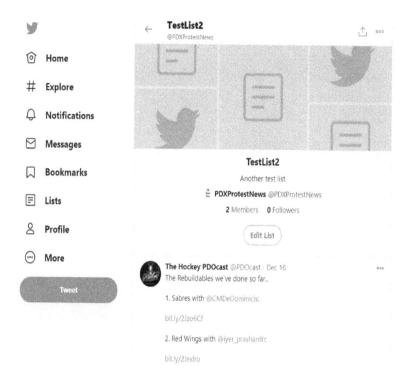

Reference: https://help.twitter.com/en/using-twitter/twitter-lists

# Setting up a RSS feed reader

Twitter lists are a good way to collect posts within the Twitter user community, but what if the people or organizations of interest do not post on Twitter? There is a wealth of information sources that publish weblogs or web sites that provide RSS feeds. A RSS feed reader can aggregate this content automatically and present in various ways, making the content available for reuse and reposting elsewhere. With the proper tools, this aggregated content itself can be displayed on the Web for anyone who has an interest in this curated stream (Appendix C describes a tool that can be used in this way). The user makes choices on the sources to follow, then the tool does the rest.

Appendix B describes how to set up the River5 feed reader, but if you want to reduce the amount of time to set up your own standalone software, you could use a web-based feed reader like Feedly. The following section will demonstrate how to use this tool.

To start an account at Feedly, go to https://feedly.com/i/welcome.

Click on the "Get Started For Free" button, a new screen will appear:

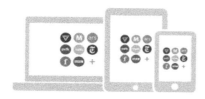

**Create an account and
access your Feedly everywhere.**

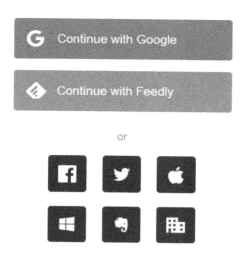

Need help logging in?

Feedly provides multiple ways to log into the service. Since the earlier section was dealing with Twitter, let us use Twitter credentials to log into Feedly. Click on the Twitter icon near the bottom of the screen. If you are already logged into Twitter, you may see the following screen.

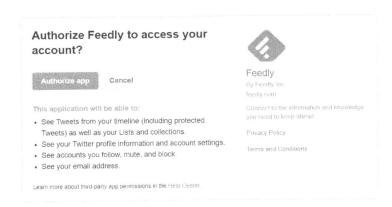

If you are not logged into Twitter, you may need to enter your Twitter username and password before getting to the "Authorize app" screen. For this example, click on the "Authorize app" button. The following screen will appear.

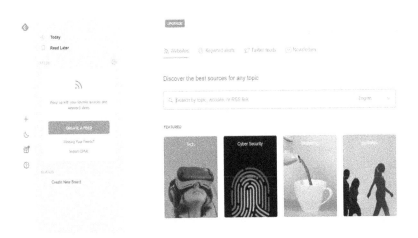

# Adding Feeds to a Feed Reader

To add a feed, you can enter a feed address in the search box, or a web site name or address. For example, entering the New York Times gives the following:

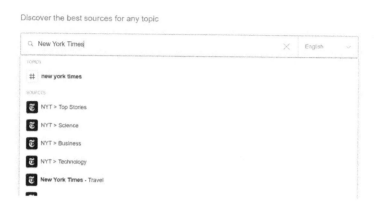

In this example, you could click on one of the Sources listed (trying NYT Top Stories gives the following).

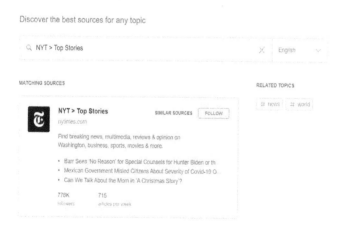

Click on the Follow button, another pop-up will appear:

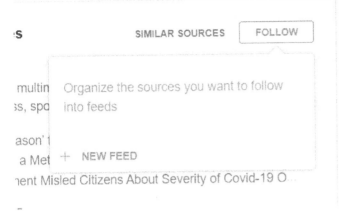

Click on "NEW FEED", another pop-up will appear.

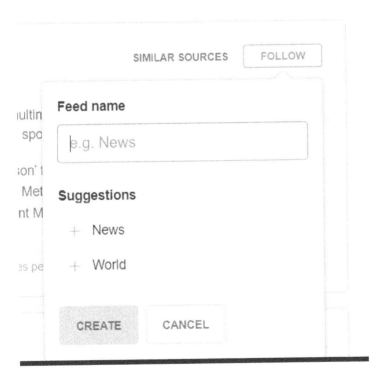

Enter a name for the overall feed group and click the Create button. The feed group will then be updated and be available on the navigation bar on the left of the screen:

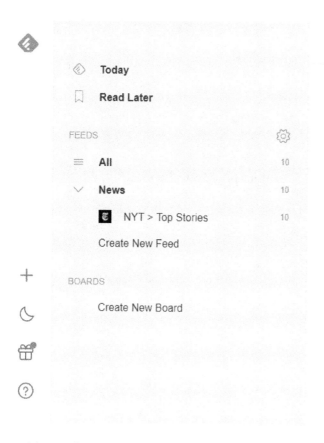

To see the stories in the NYT Top Stories feed, click on the feed name (NYT > Top Stories) in the navigation bar.

To add new sources, click on the plus sign in the left navigation bar, this will bring up the Discover page again:

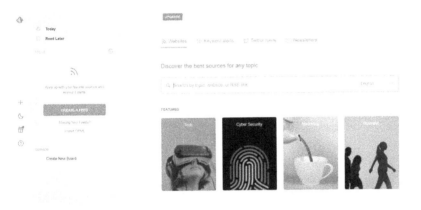

To enter a feed URL, paste the URL in the search text box:

Click on the item to bring up the next page:

Click on the Follow button, then select the feed group name created earlier (in this example, "News"):

As before, the new feed will be shown in the left navigation bar:

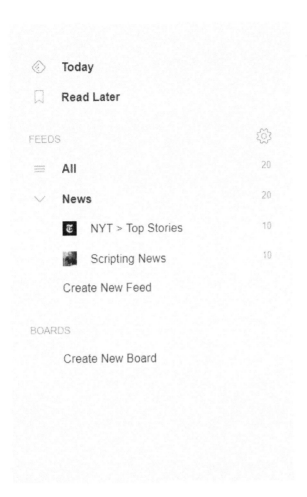

To see the new feed, click on "Scripting News" in the left navigation bar:

# Chapter 3 Setting up a WordPress Website

This chapter will show how to set up the website.

## Choose a domain name

In starting a new website, one of the big items to consider is the site domain name (URL) of the website. Things to consider are choosing a URL that is easy to remember, fits the topic of the website, and is available. Another item to consider is if the website name can fit in the length of an available Twitter handle or username. Many sites use Twitter as a communication channel for their users, so choosing a name that would work for both is worth some consideration. As an example, I decided on https://portlandprotestnews.com/ for my site URL. The maximum length of a Twitter handle is 15 characters, so this URL could not serve as the Twitter handle for the site. However, the city of Portland is commonly referred to by the initials "PDX" (the airport code for the city airport), so I decided to choose the Twitter handle "PDXProtestNews", which fit the length restriction and still was consistent with the site name. As with all things, sometimes things work out and sometimes they don't. The URL should be the primary focus, with Twitter or Facebook account names being second priority.

## Choose a domain name registrar

To reserve the domain name for your use, you will need to use a company that provides domain name registration services. A Google search

will provide a list of options, but this guide will review processes used by
https://www.namecheap.com/.

For whatever domain name registrar you choose, you will need to set up
an account and provide payment information. However, searching for
available URLs is free, and typically can be done from the site home page
(like the one above). Enter a URL (like mywonderfulsite.com) and click the
search button. You will then get a list of possible URLs:

If you happen to pick a site that is already being used, things will look
different.

# Choosing a hosting service

After purchasing a URL or domain name, the domain name service needs to know where to point the URL for the site. That information will come from the website hosting service to be used. Again, there are many hosting services available. This guide will use the formats provided by https://www.bluehost.com/.

# Assigning your domain name to the hosting services

To find the information needed, search for your hosting service, then add the words "how to set domain name servers". The following link from Bluehost (https://www.bluehost.com/help/article/modify-nameservers-other-registrars) gives the required info:

Please change your nameservers to the following Bluehost name servers:

- ns1.bluehost.com (162.88.60.37)

- ns2.bluehost.com (162.88.61.37)

Usually, the name server does not need to use the IP address (for example, 162.88.60.37), but instead uses the text form (for example, ns1.bluehost.com, ns2.bluehost.com). This page then provides a list of pages for multiple domain name registrars for how to set the name server of the registrar to point to the web hosting service. Looking at the NameCheap.com page (https://www.namecheap.com/support/knowledgebase/article.aspx/767/10/how-to-change-dns-for-a-domain/), there are several steps to take on the Namecheap.com site:

- Log into the Namecheap.com site

- Click on the Account link in the upper right corner of the screen, then select "Dashboard" from the drop-down menu

- Click on the Domain List entry in the navigation menu on the left side of the screen. This will list the domain you purchased.

- Click on the "Manage" button for that domain

- Scroll down to the Nameserver section

- Click on the drop-down arrow and select "Custom DNS"

- Enter the two nameservers provided by the web hosting company (in this example, ns1.bluehost.com and ns2.bluehost.com) in the Nameserver 1 and Nameserver2 text fields

- Click on the check mark on the right side of the screen to accept the changes.

Once you have changed a setting, the domain name registrar may require you to click "Accept" or "Make Changes" or some other action to confirm the change. After completing the change, the domain name pointers will take up to 24 hours to take effect.

## Create a draft WordPress website

After assigning the domain name to the hosting service, the next step is to create a draft WordPress site. Again, this guide will use the Bluehost hosting service as an example of how easy it is to create a WordPress site. After logging into Bluehost.com, click on the "My Sites" link in the left navigation bar:

bluehost

🏠 Home

Ⓦ **My Sites**

🛍 Marketplace

✉ Email & Office

🏢 Domains

🏪 Marketing Tools

🎛 Advanced

Next, click the "Create Site" button on the right side of the screen:

A new screen will appear:

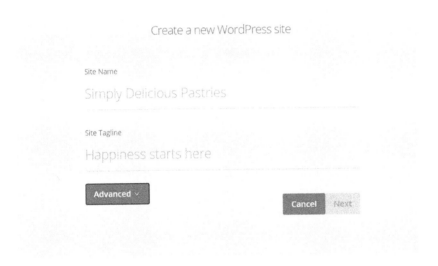

Most, if not all, WordPress themes display a name for the site at the top of the site home page and a tag line that helps to describe the site. Fill these fields in and click the Next button. If you wish, the Advanced options allow you to enter a contact email address, a site admin username, and a site admin password, but that is not required at this time (it can be set later).

After clicking the Next button, the following will appear:

For the Bluehost hosting service, all WordPress websites are created as a subdomain from the default domain website (in this case, andysylvester.com). Enter the main part of your domain name URL in the Directory text box field. For example, if your site URL was "PortlandProtestNews.com", you would enter "portlandprotestnews" without quotes in the directory. After entering a directory name, scroll down and click the "Next" button.

You will see a temp screen for a short time:

Hold tight while we set up your site.

This may take a few minutes to load.

After a period of time, the following should appear:

Congratulations, WordPress installed successfully!

Please remember your login details:

Username:     sylvester.andy
Password:     ·············  👁
Website:      https://andysylvester.com/protesttestsite
Admin:        https://andysylvester.com/protesttestsite/wp-admin

Please ensure you have securely saved your password for future access.

Go back to My Sites          Login to WordPress

Make sure to view the password and write it down or copy it in a notebook to be able to keep track. Next, click on the "Login to WordPress" link to edit some settings related to the URL.

You will see this for a short time:

Loading WordPress...

Hold on to your keyboard! You'll be there in no time!

Soon, the WordPress dashboard page should appear as follows:

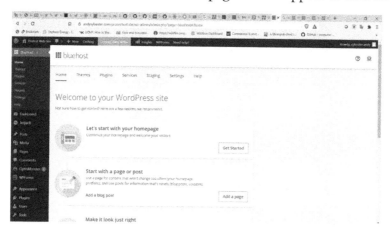

Scroll down to the Settings link in the lower part of the left navigation bar and click on that link, then select the General sub menu item from the pop-up menu (do not click on the one near the top):

Create a draft WordPress website

The page should appear as follows:

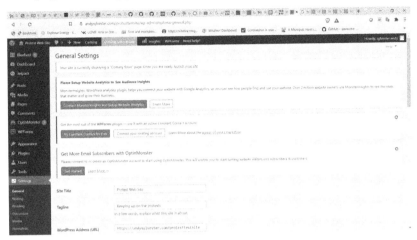

Scroll down until the WordPress Address (URL) field and the Site Address (URL) text boxes are visible:

In those two fields, enter the URL that you purchased from your domain name registrar. If your hosting provider is showing "https" at the beginning of the URL (as in the screenshot above), keep the "https" in the URL. Finally, scroll down to the bottom of the page and click the "Save Changes" button.

# Assigning your domain name to the WordPress website

Now that the domain URL has been set in the WordPress installation, the domain needs to be assigned from the Bluehost Domains page. Click the Domains link in the left navigation bar from the Bluehost account page.

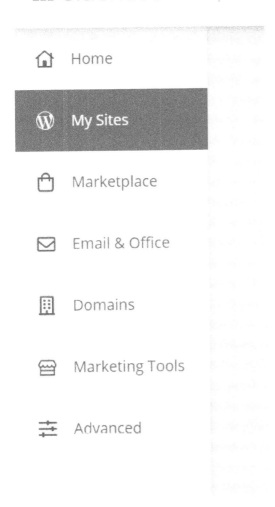

Next, click on the Subdomains sub-menu:

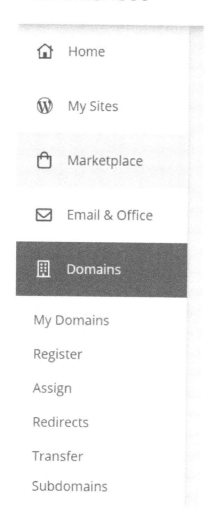

The following screen will appear:

Subdomains

Enter the name of the domain URL (for this example, "protesttestsite"), then click the Create button. The following should appear:

Subdomain Creation

Click on the "Return to Subdomains" button. This will return to the previous page. You should be able to scroll down and find the subdomain.

| portlandprotests | .andysylvester.com | ⋀/public_html/portlandprotests | not redirected | ⤴ | 🗑 |
| protesttestsite | .andysylvester.com | ⋀/public_html/protesttestsite | not redirected | ⤴ | 🗑 |

Now, go back to the navigation menu and select the "Assign" link.

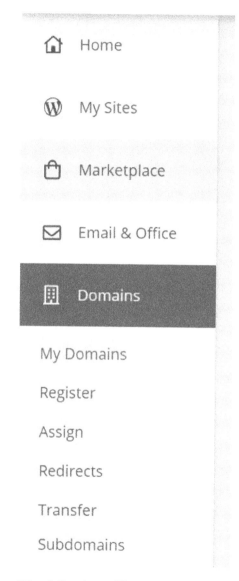

My Domains

Register

Assign

Redirects

Transfer

Subdomains

The following will appear:

Assigning your domain name to the WordPress website

## Assign Domain

For Step 1, click on the radio button for "Use a domain that is not already associated with your account." Enter the main part of the domain URL without the "https://" (for example, "protesttestsite.com").

Step 2 is to verify your ownership of the site:

If you have updated the nameserver URLs with your domain name registrar, this display should change within 5-10 seconds to show that the hosting service has verified that you own the domain.

Step 3 is to select which type of domain to assign:

Select the Addon Domain radio button.

In Step 4, you will select the subdirectory that the domain will point to:

Earlier, you created the directory for your WordPress site. Click the "Use an existing directory" radio button and select the directory name created earlier in this section. Finally, click the "Assign this Domain" button. A success screen will appear. Within 5-10 minutes, the WordPress site will be available at the new domain name.

References:

https://www.bluehost.com/blog/how-create-wordpress-website-5-quick-steps/

https://www.bluehost.com/blog/how-to-make-a-wordpress-website-bluehost/

https://www.bluehost.com/help/article/subdomains

https://www.bluehost.com/help/article/how-to-assign-a-domain

## Site setup checklist

Now that the WordPress site has been created, several settings should be updated to prepare the site to go live. The first is to update the auto generated password that was created when the site was created. Go back to the site dashboard page, then click on the Users link in the left navigation bar, then select the All Users sub menu. The following will appear:

Click on the user marked as Administrator (when a WordPress site is created using the one-click tools in Bluehost, it assigns an administrator based on the login and email credentials of the account holder). A page will appear with many options for changing user attributes. Scroll down to the bottom of the page and find the Account Management section.

Click on the "Set New Password" button. The following will appear:

Erase the text in the text box and replace it with a password of your choosing. The page will provide an assessment of the strength of the password. When you have entered the new password, click the "Update Profile" button at the bottom of the page. After the page refreshes, the password will have been updated. To check this, you can log out of the site and log back in to see that the new password has taken effect.

The next option to update is the site time zone. The default is UTC +0, which is equivalent to Greenwich Mean Time. It is a good practice to change the time zone to the one where you live (to avoid posts appearing to be on the next day). Go back to the site dashboard page, then click on the Settings link in the left navigation bar, then select the General sub menu. The following will appear:

Scroll down to the time zone section of the page:

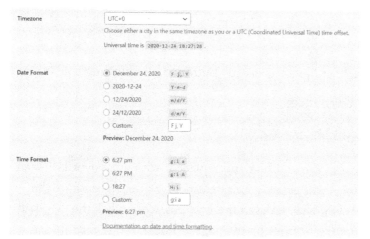

Click on the drop-down in the Timezone area and select a city within your time zone. You can also change the default date/time format as well. When you have finished your selections, scroll down to the bottom of the page and click the "Save Changes" button.

Another good practice is to change the URL format for weblog posts to be based on the title of the post. The default includes the post number in the URL, which is not very descriptive. Go back to the site dashboard page, then click on the Settings link in the left navigation bar, then select the Permalinks sub menu. The following will appear:

Click on the Post Name radio button, then scroll down to the bottom of the page and click the "Save Changes" button.

# Choose a theme

The next major decision for the web site is to choose a theme. WordPress provides several themes with the basic installation (currently three themes for 2019, 2020, and 2021 at the writing of this guide). You can certainly start with any of these themes, but it is a good idea to think about the planned "look and feel" of the site. For PortlandProtestNews.com, the goal was to have a "news site" look. After searching "free wordpress themes news site", I eventually found the Mission News theme (https://www.competethemes.com/mission-news/), which was free and had the desired look. Once you have located a theme that meets your design goals, here is how to add it to your website. Go back to the site Dashboard page, then click on the Appearance link in the left navigation bar, then select the Themes sub menu. The following will appear:

To add a new theme to the set of available themes, click on the Upload button at the top of the window. The following will appear:

Enter the name of the desired theme in the "Search themes…." text box and press the Enter key. For this example, entering "mission news" brings up the following:

Hover over the thumbnail image of the theme, then click on the Install button that will appear. After a few seconds, the following will appear:

Click the Activate button to make this theme the active theme when the site goes live.

# Making your first post

Now, it is time to start thinking about the structure of posts to the site and how frequently new material will be posted. Will the frequency of posts be daily, weekly, or some other period? Also, will the posts have the same structure, or will they vary in content? Some sites provide links, links with quotes from the post being linked, news, analysis, and/or opinion. Original material could be long or short form posts. The content of posts to the site do not all have to be the same, but some thought should be given to what will be posted. You might want to consider creating an editorial calendar as a structure to guide creation of content. For example, there might be a weekly spotlight feature on a person of interest in your topic, or a roundup of the top stories of the week.

After answering the questions in the previous paragraph, you should be ready to create your first post. To start, go to the Dashboard page and click the Posts link in the left navigation bar. The following will appear:

When a new WordPress site is created, a dummy first post is created with the title "Hello World!". This is the post that was shown when the site went live. This dummy post can be edited or deleted. To create a new post, click the "Add New" link in the left navigation bar. The following will appear:

The editor interface in WordPress is now called a "block editor". The interface has a set of "blocks" that represent types of content that can be included in a post. The default above is a Paragraph block, which allows the user to start typing text as soon as the new post has been created in the editor. The following is an example:

When you have reached the end of the paragraph and press the Enter key, the editor will create a new Paragraph block for the next part of the post.

The black plus on the right side of the screen allows the user to select different types of blocks.

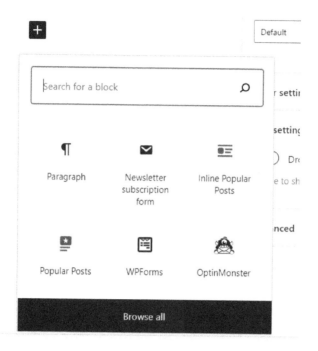

Click on the "Browse all" link at the bottom to see a list of available blocks on the left side of the screen.

To add a YouTube video to a post, scroll down to the Video block and click on it:

The following pop-up will appear:

To embed a YouTube video, click on the "Insert from URL" link. A popup with a text box will appear. Enter the URL and press the Enter key. The video should then appear as embedded in the post:

To change the alignment, click on the middle box in the bar above the video to change the alignment to left, center or right. The center alignment looks as follows:

When the post is complete, click on the Preview link in the upper right corner of the screen, then select the "Desktop" option, then select the "Preview in new tab" menu item:

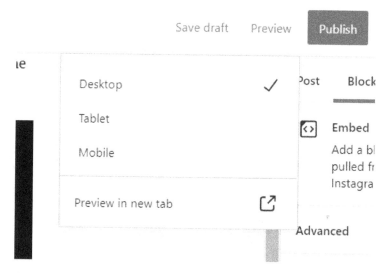

After several seconds, the post should appear in a new browser tab:

To publish the post to the site, click back to the editor tab and click on the "Publish" button in the upper left corner of the screen. A dialog will appear asking to you confirm that you want to publish the post:

Click the Publish button again. The following will appear:

Click on the View post button on the right side of the screen to view the post on the site:

In the browser address bar, note that the URL is based on the title of the post, as this was the setting selected earlier in this guide.

If you perform a refresh of the site, you should see the following:

In this view, the first post is not fully displayed. The Mission News theme defaults to displaying the first 30 words of a post on the home page. To change this to allow full posts on the home page, go back to the Dashboard page, then click the Appearance menu item, then the Customize sub-menu item. The following screen will appear:

On the left navigation bar, click on the Excerpts menu. The following will appear:

Customizing

# Excerpts

**Show full posts on blog?**

○ Yes

⦿ No

**Excerpt word count**

30

Click the Yes radio button. The screen will update as follows:

The full post can now be seen. Click on the Publish button to accept the changes. When the button text changes to "Published", the changes are complete. Click the "x" in the upper left corner of the screen to return to the Dashboard.

For more information on using the block editor in WordPress, see the following resources:

https://www.wpbeginner.com/beginners-guide/how-to-use-the-new-wordpress-block-editor/

https://www.codeinwp.com/blog/wordpress-gutenberg-guide/

https://wordpress.org/support/article/first-steps-with-wordpress/

https://wordpress.org/support/article/wordpress-editor/

# Make your site live

Up to this point, the site has not been live. To make it easier to see future customizing, it is time to push the site to a live state. Go to the Dashboard page for the site, then click on the "Coming Soon Active" area at the top of the screen (shown below):

Once the screen updates, scroll down to the bottom and click the "Launch Your Site" button as shown below:

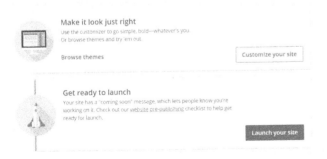

After a few seconds, this will update to the following:

**Awesome! Your site is live.**
We removed the "coming soon" banner. Your website is now available for
public visitors. This can be always be changed on the Settings tab above.

Restore Coming Soon

To view your site, go up to the upper left corner of the window where
the site name is displayed ("Protest Web Site" in this example), click on the
site name, then select the "Visit Site" pop-up menu. The site will then be
displayed:

A more complete reference for getting started with customizing the
Mission News theme can be found at https://support.competethemes.com/
help/getting-started-mission-news/.

# Chapter 4 - Adding social media support

## Decide what to post on social media

Chapter 3 briefly talked about what type of material to post on your website. Assuming that you will have some type of social media associated with the website, you should think about how to use social media to drive people to your website. For the Portland Protest News site, the primary use of social media was Twitter, and posts were a one-line summary of the daily post to the website. Of course, other types of material could be posted to social media. The important thing is to consider your goals for the website and social media and let that guide your posting.

## Adding social media links to your website

There are many aspects of the Mission News theme that can be customized. Here are instructions for adding links to social media accounts. To start, go to the Dashboard for the site, then click the Themes menu item, then click the Customize sub-menu item. The following will appear:

To add links to social media accounts, click on the Social Media Icons menu item on the left menu bar. The following will appear in the menu bar.

Add URLs for a Twitter account and a Youtube channel. As text is added to the form, icons for those accounts will appear in the upper right corner of the site page and at the center of the bottom of the page. In addition, the "Published" button at the top of the menu will change text to "Publish" and the button will become active. When you have finished entering the account URLs, click the "Publish" button in the form. To close the Customize menu, click the "x" in the upper left corner of the menu form.

A more complete reference for getting started with customizing the Mission News theme can be found at https://support.competethemes.com/help/getting-started-mission-news/.

# Chapter 5 - Adding a newsletter

## Choose a service or plugin

Many sites offer a way to receive the site content by email. There are many plugins for WordPress weblogs that offer re-packaging of the posted content, but in some ways an email newsletter provides the best control over how your content is presented. Of the free email newsletter services, MailChimp (https://mailchimp.com/) is attractive, but the free plan only allows one newsletter. For starting out, it is possible to use a free WordPress plugin to support creating and sending newsletters. An excellent one is called The Newsletter Plugin (https://www.thenewsletterplugin.com/). This section of the guide will show how to install this plugin and go through the basic steps of creating a newsletter.

## Example - Installing The Newsletter Plugin

### Setup

Go to the site dashboard page, then click on the Plugins link in the left navigation bar. The following will appear:

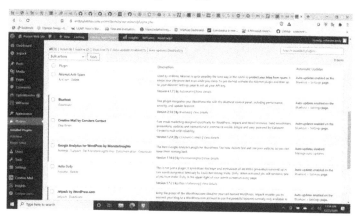

The typical WordPress install will contain a number of plugins (Akismet Anti-Spam, Hello Dolly, etc.) along with others added by the hosting provider. As the site owner, you can use as few or as many plugins as you like. To add a new plugin, the easiest way is to perform a plugin search. On the site dashboard page, click on the Add New link below the Plugins link in the left navigation bar. The following will appear:

For this example, enter the text "Newsletter Free" in the Search plugins text box. This will return a number of plugins with those two words in the title/description:

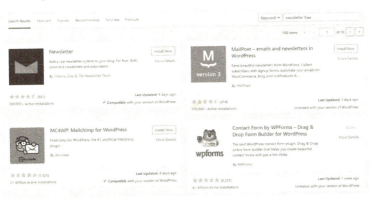

For this example, click on the "Install Now" button on the box titled "Newsletter" with the black and red logo. After five to ten seconds, the "Install Now" button will change to "Activate". Click the "Activate" button. After five to ten seconds, a new screen will appear:

Click the "Next" button to go through a guided set of steps to initialize settings for this plugin. You can always update the settings at a later time.

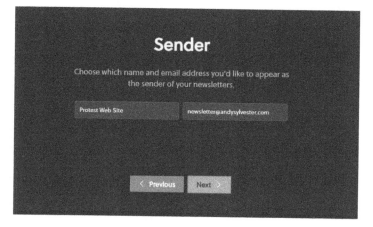

Update the text fields if needed, then click the "Next" button.

These settings affect the appearance of a subscription form to be added to your website. The default settings are to just display a Subscribe button. Make any changes needed and click the "Next" button.

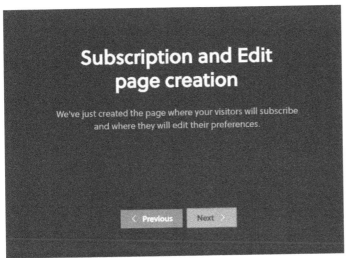

There is no action that needs to be taken on this page, click the "Next" button to continue.

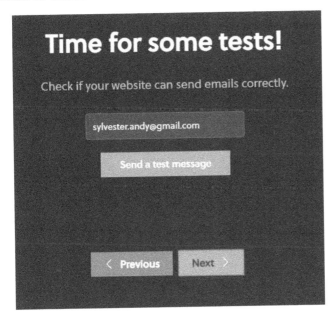

Sending a test message is a good way to demonstrate that the mail send features are working correctly. You can use the default email address or supply a different address, then click the "Send a test message" button. Click the "Next" button to continue.

## Creating a subscription form

Most WordPress themes divide the main page into several sections, with the main content in the middle of the page, with a left and/or right section next to the content. These sections are typically called "sidebars", and can provide additional support for navigating the site. The Newsletter plugin can add a "widget" which contains a form for signing up for the newsletter. To add the basic widget, click the "Take me to my widget settings" button. A new browser tab will open with the following:

The Mission News website theme has both a left and a right sidebar. For this example, click on the Newsletter dropdown in the Available Widgets section and select "Right Sidebar", then click the "Add Widget" button.

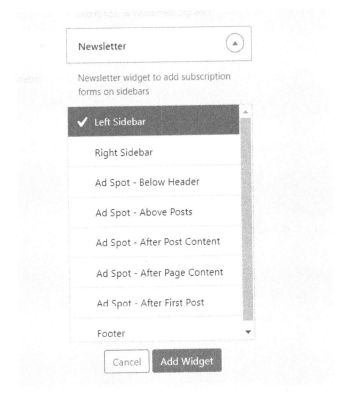

A form will appear in the Right Sidebar area on the right side of the window.

For this example, enter the text "Sign up to get email updates!" in the Title text box, then click the "Save" button at the bottom of the form, then click the drop-down arrow to collapse the form. Return to the Newsletter setup browser tab and click the Next button. The following will appear.

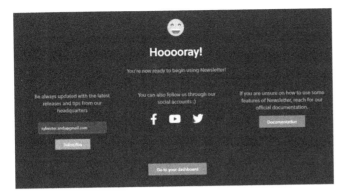

Click the "Go to your dashboard" button, the following will appear.

To see how the subscription form looks on the site, go up to the upper left corner of the window where the site name is displayed ("Protest Web Site" in this example), click on the site name, then select the "Visit Site" pop-up menu. The site will then be displayed, the subscription form will be on the right sidebar:

Chapter 5 - Adding a newsletter

Reference: http://andysylvester.com/2020/09/12/choosing-a-mailing-list-tool-for-wordpress-besides-mailchimp

## Creating and sending out newsletters

From the Dashboard shown above, click on the "Newsletters" menu, then select the "Create Newsletter" menu item. The following will appear:

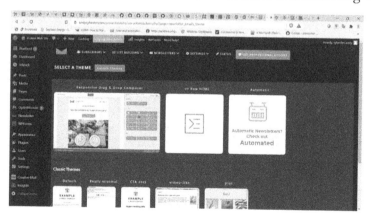

There are multiple themes available for formatting newsletters, as shown above. For this example, the "Responsive Drag & Drop Composer" will be

used. Click on the image below "Responsive Drag & Drop Composer". The following will appear:

On the left side of the screen, several preset newsletter structures are shown. On the right side, design elements for the header, content, and footer of the newsletter are shown. For this example, a blank preset will be used. Scroll down on the left side of the screen and click on the "Start with an empty project" icon.

The editor screen will update as follows:

Enter a subject line in the "Newsletter subject" text box in the upper left corner of the editor. If you are sending content from a blog post, you might use the title of the blog post as the subject line. Next, click on the Header block on the right side of the editor and drag it into the editing field. The following will appear:

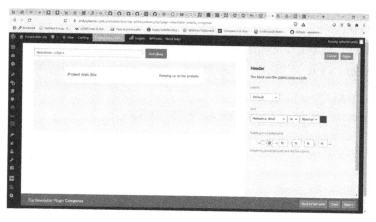

In this example, the header automatically puts the website title and tag line into the header. If this is acceptable, click the "Apply" button in the upper right corner. The blocks editor will reappear on the right side of the window.

To add text to the email, click on the "Text" block on the right side of the window and drag it into the editor space. The following will appear:

On the right side of the screen, the default text is shown in a text editor, and shown in the newsletter view on the left side of the screen. To start editing, delete the default text in the editor and add text of your own, including styling and links. When you are finished, click the Apply button to see the text in the newsletter view.

If you need to do further editing, hover on the right side of the body portion of the newsletter view. Click the ruler and pencil icon (left of three icons) to resume editing.

To complete the newsletter, scroll to the bottom of the blocks view on the right side of the window, click on the "Footer" block and drag it into the newsletter view. The following will appear:

To accept the footer, click the "Apply" button in the upper right corner of the screen. Click the "Save" button in the bottom right corner, then after the screen updates, click the "Next" button. The following will appear.

To send the newsletter immediately, click the "Send now" button at the top of the screen. A pop-up will appear asking you to confirm that you wish to send the newsletter.

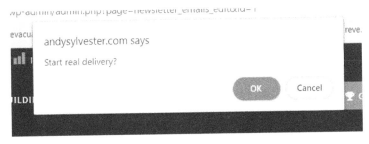

Click OK, then the delivery will start as shown below.

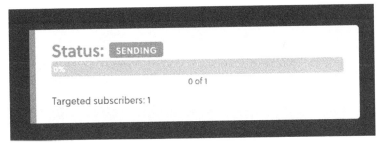

When the sending is complete, the following will be displayed (you will have to refresh the screen to see it):

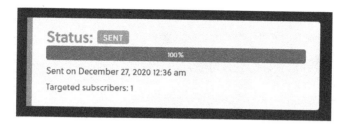

# Chapter 6 - Define Your Workflow

If you have worked through this guide up to this point, you should have the following:

- A RSS feed reader account and a list of sources to bring news and information to you on the topic your site will cover.

- A Twitter list with similar sources not available via RSS

- A working WordPress site with a permanent URL

- A newsletter plugin that can collect email addresses, help you create and send email newsletters to people that want them

This guide has covered three types of posting (weblog/website, social media, and newsletter). Once you have decided on a posting frequency, it is good to develop a workflow for creating the content you will be posting. As an example, here was the general workflow used for the Portland Protest News site.

General workflow

- Post daily to weblog, social media, and newsletter (social media is summary of weblog with pointer to weblog post, newsletter is same content as weblog post and is in HTML format)

Weblog post workflow

- Review RSS reader feeds for posts/stories related to protests, open tabs for each post that looks interesting

- Review tabs, choose the posts that are most applicable to the goals of the site, delete tabs that do not apply or are duplicates of the other posts

- Open a new post on the weblog, start adding links to posts/stories (link text is to source of post/story (identifies source, like "New

York Times")), copy headline of story and perhaps sub-headline (if any)

- For Twitter posts, get embed code and add to weblog post

- At the top of the post, write a one-sentence summary of the items included in the daily post

- Preview the post to look for grammar/spelling errors, make any revisions needed

- Add categories (news, videos)

- Publish the post, review on the site

Social media workflow

- Copy one sentence summary from the weblog post into the tweet text area

- Add link to weblog post

- Edit text if needed to fit within tweet length limit

- Post tweet

Newsletter workflow

- Bring up daily post in weblog editor

- Copy text of post

- Paste text into text editor (will be HTML)

- For Twitter posts, get embed code and add to text editor

- Add align element to paragraph tag to make content left-justified (<p align="left">)

- Create new newsletter, add header and HTML elements

- Add content from text editor to HTML element and save

- Add footer element

- Preview newsletter

- Send newsletter

If the site is a single-person operation, this may be too detailed. However, if more than one person is participating, having a defined workflow can help in maintaining consistency while dividing the work among several people.

# Chapter 7 - Next Steps

By following this guide, you have set up tools to collect information on a topic of your choice, created a website focused on this topic, and set up a newsletter and social media accounts to support your website. Congratulations! You can definitely stop at this point with the tools you have. However, there are other tools and technologies that can help you in your journey to follow your topic and provide the latest information related to that topic. The appendices that follow (setting up your own server, setting up your own feed reader, setting up web pages to display rivers of news, getting a Twitter development account, and running server tools that process data from Twitter) are more advanced that the main part of this guide, but can provide freedom and more control over your toolset than using free tools or tools provided by other services. The choice is up to you!

# Appendix A - Setting Up A Virtual Server

## Setting up a server - why do it?

For many people, using the Internet means using existing services to collect, publish, and consume content. Most of these services are free to use or are supported through advertising. There is nothing wrong with using free services or products, but users should realize there are costs, even though they may not be direct. For ad-supported services, you are the product being sold. For other free services, the content that you contribute can be hard to get back, and may not be retrievable at all (or could disappear if the services were to go away). For these reasons and many others, it is a good skill to be able to set up a virtual server and run your own applications and services. In this way, you control the tools and make them do what you want. You own the data and are not dependent on some other person or company. The cost can be as little as $5/month, and can stopped at any time. So why not give it a try?

## Setting up a server - where to get one?

There are many companies providing virtual server hosting. This guide will focus on one provider, Digital Ocean (https://www.digitalocean.com/), which offers a $5/month plan to get started. The first step is to sign up by going to the website listed above:

Click on the "Sign Up" button in the upper left corner of the window. The following screen will appear:

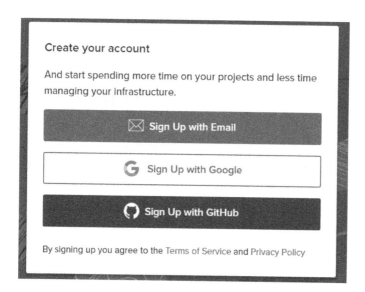

This example will demonstrate how to sign up with an email account (could be a GMail account, but will use the generic email signup). Click on the "Sign Up with Email" button, the following will appear:

Enter the information listed, then click the "Sign Up" button. The following will appear:

Check your email inbox for a verification email. In the email, there will be a link from Digital Ocean. Click on the link, a new web page will open with the following:

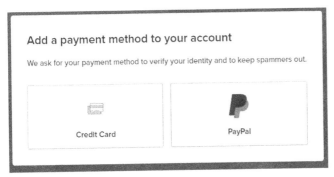

Click on the "Credit Card" button, then fill out information for billing to your credit card. After you save the payment method, the following will appear:

Appendix A - Setting Up A Virtual Server

Click on the "Let's make something" button to get started on creating a server.

# Creating the virtual server

Digital Ocean calls its virtual servers "Droplets" (cute, eh?). A user can choose to create a Droplet with certain tools/applications already installed. This example will create a new Ubuntu Droplet and perform manual setup of tools to access the server. Ubuntu is a common Linux distribution for virtual servers and will be used in this example.

The following screen shows your Dashboard:

Click on the "Get Started with a Droplet" button. The following will appear:

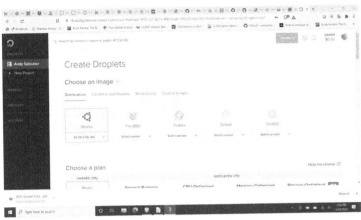

The first step is to choose a Linux distribution that will run on the server. For this example, we will choose the Ubuntu image. Accept the default operating system version, it will always show the latest one.

Scroll down to the next section:

For this example, choose the Basic CPU option and the $5/month charge. This is sufficient to get started, and you can always increase the power of your Droplet at a later time.

Scroll down to the next section:

Appendix A - Setting Up A Virtual Server

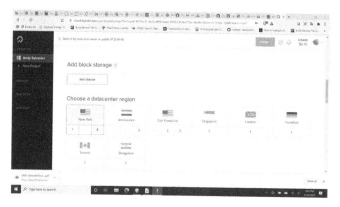

Do not select anything on the "Add block storage" option. For the "Choose a datacenter region", select a region that is closest to your physical location.

Scroll down to the next section:

Leave the default setting for the VPC Network, and do not check anything at this time in the "Select additional options" section.

Scroll down to the next section:

In the Authentication section, select the "Password" method of authentication, then enter a password in the "Create root password" text box. Please note the password requirements below, you will not be allowed to create the Droplet unless your password meets those requirements.

Using SSH keys is a more secure method of authentication, but requires the creation of the keys prior to creating the server, so password access is easier to start with. More information on using SSH keys will be included at the end of the appendix.

Scroll down to the next section:

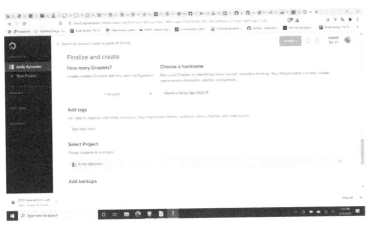

For this example, select "1 Droplet" from the "How many Droplets? dropdown box, leave the "Choose a hostname" text box as-is, do not enter any text in the "Add tags" text box, and do not click anything in the Select Project area (the droplet will be assigned to your account).

Scroll down to the final section:

Do not click the checkbox for enabling backups at this time, this can be added at a later date. Click on the "Create Droplet" bar in the middle of the screen. The following will appear:

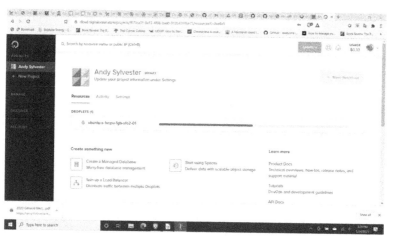

Once the thermometer scale reaches the right side of the screen, the thermometer will be removed and a IP address should be visible as follows:

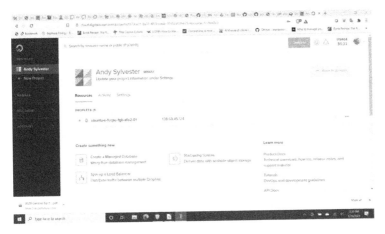

Write down the IP address for later use.

For more information and options on how to create a Droplet on Digital Ocean, see the following article:

https://www.digitalocean.com/docs/droplets/how-to/create/

The Droplet creation is now complete, and it is ready for use. To check out logging into the Droplet from this screen, click on the three dots on the right side of the screen. A set of options will appear in a drop-down menu:

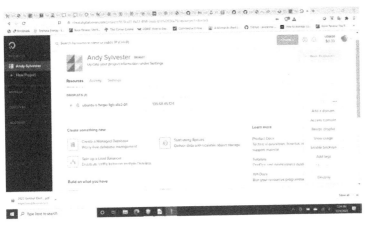

Click on the "Access console" menu item. The following window will appear:

Enter the word "root" without quotes, then press the Enter key. A new line will be displayed asking for a password:

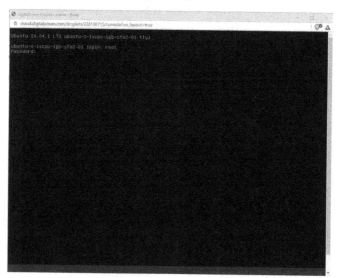

Enter the password that you entered when creating the Droplet. The following will then appear:

You can now access the server and install applications (this will be covered in later appendices). If you wish to use a standalone application to log into the server, the Terminal app for Macintosh or the Putty application for Windows are good choices. Here are some links on setting up and using these applications:

Using Terminal app for Macintosh users:

https://www.digitalocean.com/docs/droplets/how-to/connect-with-ssh/openssh/

Download for Putty for Windows:

https://www.ssh.com/ssh/putty/download

Installation for Putty for Windows:

https://www.ssh.com/ssh/putty/windows/install

Using Putty:

https://www.ssh.com/ssh/putty/windows/

Putty user manual:

https://the.earth.li/~sgtatham/putty/0.74/htmldoc/

Putty home page:

https://www.chiark.greenend.org.uk/~sgtatham/putty/

In addition to accessing your server using a terminal application, you will need to be able to transfer files to your server using a File Transfer Protocol (FTP) application. A popular free and open source application is the FileZilla FTP client. The following pages include installation instructions and a tutorial for using FileZilla on Macintosh or Windows:

https://wiki.filezilla-project.org/Client_Installation

https://wiki.filezilla-project.org/FileZilla_Client_Tutorial_(en)

# SSH key information

The following article is an overview on how to create and add SSH keys to your Digital Ocean droplet to use those keys when you log into your server using a terminal window (Mac) or Putty (Windows). This is another option for logging in besides entering a username and password combination.

https://www.digitalocean.com/docs/droplets/how-to/add-ssh-keys/

The following article shows how Macintosh users can create SSH keys using OpenSSH:

https://www.digitalocean.com/docs/droplets/how-to/add-ssh-keys/create-with-openssh/

The following article shows how Windows users can create SSH keys using Putty:

https://www.digitalocean.com/docs/droplets/how-to/add-ssh-keys/create-with-putty/

The following article shows how to connect for Macintosh users:

https://www.digitalocean.com/docs/droplets/how-to/connect-with-ssh/openssh/

The following article shows how to connect for Windows users using Putty

https://www.digitalocean.com/docs/droplets/how-to/connect-with-ssh/putty/

The following article shows how to use the Filezilla application to transfer files to the server using File Transfer Protocol (FTP) and SSH keys:

https://www.digitalocean.com/docs/droplets/how-to/transfer-files/

Another useful article:

https://medium.com/@filjoseph/how-to-connect-to-your-digital-ocean-droplet-56c15d7675c9

# Appendix B - Setting up River5 feed aggregator

The Ubuntu server image has a number of tools installed, but no applications. This appendix will demonstrate how to add tools for running applications using the Node.js framework (https://nodejs.org/en/) , and how to install and run a Node.js application.

Log into your server using a Mac terminal window or the Putty app on Windows or through the Digital Ocean dashboard (see Appendix A for instructions), then type the following commands in the terminal window to install the following packages (press Enter at the end of each command):

sudo apt-get install nodejs

sudo apt-get install npm

sudo apt-get install nodejs-legacy

When these commands are entered, the server may list the storage space required for the packages, as shown below:

Press Y and then Enter to continue the installation.

After these installations are complete, the Node module called "forever" should be installed using the Node Package Manager (NPM). This will be used later to keep the application running when you are not logged into the server. Enter the following command in the terminal window:

sudo npm install forever -g

Next, the Git configuration management software should be installed. The demo application is stored using the Github service, which uses Git to manage the files. Enter the following command in the terminal window:

sudo apt-get install git

Now that you have Node.js, NPM and Git installed, an easy first Node.js application to install is the River5 feed reader/aggregator by Dave Winer. Its key features are:

- Ability to group feeds together (subscription lists)

- Display of grouped feeds in reverse-chronological order

- Display of feeds is integrated (feeds not displayed by feed, but by time, resulting in a mix of feed items)

- Can use River5 locally (desktop/laptop, PC/Mac/Linux) or hosted (Linux)

- Can view feeds online (River5 port 1337)

- Can take output of River5 (river files) and display them using different templates (single or multiple rivers) (covered in Appendix C)

## Installation

To start the River5 installation, enter the following command in the terminal window:

git clone https://github.com/scripting/river5.git

This command creates a copy of the River5 RSS aggregator on the server. Type the following command in the terminal window:

ls -l

Note that the command has two lower-case letter L's. This command will list the directory contents. The following text should appear:

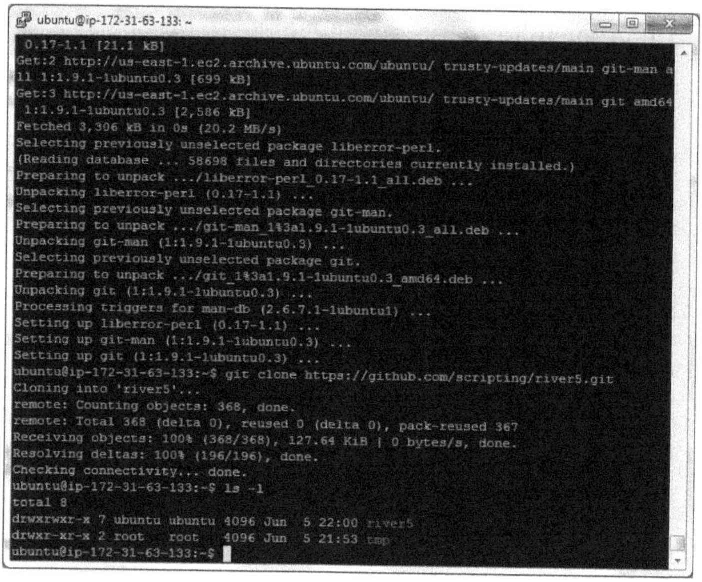

Enter the following command to change directory to the river5 directory.

cd river5

Next, enter the following command to install the required Node packages for the River5 app:

sudo npm install

Text will be scrolling for 10-15 seconds. Finally, enter this command:

node river5.js

This starts the River5 application. The default installation includes a set of five lists of feeds (more on this in a later section), which River5 will fetch and process. A long list of article titles will scroll by, then the scrolling should stop.

Open a browser tab to the URL or IP address of your server with ":1337" (port 1337) added to the end (for example: http://fedwiki.andysylvester.com:1337/ or http://134.234.154.64:1337 )

You should see a list of tabs displaying news articles:

Click on the Nyt tab to see a list of articles from the New York Times:

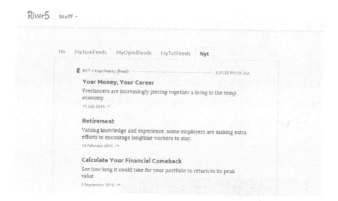

The tab names correspond to the filenames of the files containing the feed URLs. This will be described more in a later section.

Type Control-C in the terminal window to stop the application.

# Keeping River5 running continuously

In the above section, River5 was started manually, and ran until stopped with the Control-C command. It would also have stopped when the terminal window was closed. To keep River5 running continuously, another application must be used. The forever Node application was installed earlier in this appendix. Using forever allows a Node.js application to continue running without the terminal window being active. To start River5 using forever, enter the following command in the river5 directory:

forever -o out.log -e err.log start river5.js

This form of the command sends terminal output from River5 to out.log, and any errors upon ending the forever process to err.log. If you do not wish to collect any information on the application or errors, the command can be shortened as follows:

forever start river5.js

# Creating feed lists for River5

The way to add feeds or feed lists for River5 to collect is through the use of standalone text files. These files need to be uploaded to the server using a File Transfer Protocol (FTP) application. Appendix A provides instructions on setting up the Filezilla FTP app.

There are three file formats that can be used:

- Plain text files

- OPML files (Outliner Processor Markup Language) (see http://dev.opml.org/ for more information on the format)

- JSON files (Javascript Object Notation) (see https://www.json.org/json-en.html for more information on the format)

For the plain text file format, all that is required is to create a text file with feed URLs on single lines. The example file in River5 can be found in the river5/lists folder within the river5 installation on the server, file myTxtFeeds.txt. In this example, the filename without the file extension will be the name of the tab in the River5 display (myTxtFeeds).

For the OPML file format, there are two common ways of creating the file. The first is by using an outliner that creates OPML files. The Little Outliner web application by Dave Winer (http://littleoutliner.com/) is available online, and several other outlining applications export data in OPML format. The following instructions for the Fargo outline editor (http://river4.smallpict.com/2015/08/04/editingSubscriptionLists.html) are applicable to Little Outliner. A video demonstrating this application can be found at https://www.youtube.com/watch?v=VET958_s2hc. The second common way is to export an OPML subscription list from a RSS feed reader (many feed readers provide this feature). The example files in River5 can be found in the river5/lists folder, files myOPMLFeeds.opml, and nyt.opml. These example files could also be edited in a text editor to add or replace existing feeds. In this example, the filenames without the file extension will be the name of the corresponding tabs in the River5 display (myOPMLFeeds, nyt).

For the JSON format, create a text file with the extension .json (for example, feeds.json). In the file, add each feed URL on a separate line. Make sure to have a comma at the end of each line except the last one. Here is an example:

```
[
"http://feeds.feedburner.com/nymag/intel",
"http://radio3.io/users/davewiner/rss.xml",
"http://www.schockwellenreiter.de/feed/",
"http://feed.dilbert.com/dilbert/blog",
"http://www.npr.org/rss/rss.php?id=1145",
"http://www.npr.org/rss/rss.php?id=1040"
]
```

Note that each feed is in quotes, there is a comma at the end of each line, except for the last feed, and that there is an open bracket ([) at the top of the file and a close bracket (]) at the end of the file. Source: https://github.com/scripting/river5/blob/master/lists/myJsonFeeds.json

A feature of River5 is that any number of feed list files can be created and displayed. Each list will be displayed in a different tab. This is an excellent way to group feed by topic and make it easier to follow news on a given topic.

## Stopping River5 running under forever

Enter the following command in the river5 directory:

forever stopall

# Stopping River5 manually

Enter Control-C to stop River5 if running the app manually (not using the forever command)

# Checking on River5 status

- Log into Digital Ocean server, change directory to river5

- Type "forever list" to confirm if there are no forever processes running. If there is no process running, go to the next step.

- Enter "ls -l" to get listing of files/folders in river5 folder

- If the following command was used to start River5 (forever -o out.log -e err.log start river5.js), check the file err.log. If the file err.log has 0 bytes, River5 is running without problems

- If the file err.log has more than 0 bytes, recommend reviewing the file in an editor or downloading it for review.

# Troubleshooting tips

1. River items not updating

    a. Check to see if forever command is still running

    b. Look at river5/rivers folder to see if river files are being updated (*.js files)

2. Added new feeds to a subscription file, but have not seen anything in River5

    a. River5 reads a feed when it is added, and does not start adding items from the feed to the river until the feed updates after the initial read. If the feed updates once a day, you may not see anything for a while.

    b. Look at log file for error messages related to that feed

3. Cannot access River5 display on port 1337

    a. Check to see if River5 is running

    b. Check to see if forever command is still running (for hosted/Linux installs)

    c. Make sure that the main URL is correct

# References

For more information on using River5, see the Github page at https://github.com/scripting/river5.

http://river4.smallpict.com/ - River4 weblog, has a number of tips that apply to River5

# Appendix C - Setting up Rivers of News

In the same vein as "own your data" or "supporting the open web", it's important for users to be able to set up their own tools for collecting/reading information on the Web, and not be dependent on other people's tools. An example is the river of news I have set up for my own reading (http://readinglist.andysylvester.com/). This is a display of a list of news items in reverse-chronologic order. Dave Winer gives a more detailed explanation at http://scripting.com/2014/06/02/whatIsARiverOfNewsAggregator.html. This appendix will help you to do the same for any blogs/feeds that you are interested in following.

There are two pieces to the river resource given above:

1. An installation of the River5 RSS aggregator by Dave Winer running on a server (server setup is covered in Appendix A, River5 setup is covered in Appendix B)

2. An HTML page served from a web hosting account that displays a river or rivers created by River5

Once you have River5 set up on a public server and creating river files (Javascript files that can be read/displayed by other applications (for example, 1999bloggers.js)), you have some options for being able to display those files. When River5 is running, you can direct people to the public display of the rivers being created. An example can be seen at http://fedwiki.andysylvester.com:1337, which is my main River5 installation. This install is creating multiple rivers, which are displayed in multiple tabs. If you only had one river, you would see only one tab.

Another option for making your river public without pointing to the River5 app display is to use a separate HTML page that accesses the river files. Dave Winer has created a toolkit for display of River5 river files (https://github.com/scripting/riverBrowser). To test the app, copy two files from the repo (frozenriver.js and riverbrowserdemo.html) to a directory on a web server. You should then see the contents of the frozen river file as shown in Dave Winer's demo app (http://fargo.io/code/browsers/riverbrowserdemo.html).

To set up your own public display of a River5 river, make a copy of the riverbrowserdemo.html file in the Github repo mentioned above. Next, open the file in a text editor and find the line with the phrase "httpGetRiver". It should look like this:

httpGetRiver("frozenriver.js", "idRiverDisplay", function () {

Next, you will be replacing the text "frozenriver.js" with a URL to a list in your River5 installation. For example, I have a file called readinglist.txt, which contains a list of over 40 RSS feeds that I follow. When your River5 installation is running, you can feed a URL corresponding to a River5 list of feeds that you have created (some examples can be found at https://github.com/scripting/river5#examples-of-lists). The following is the line of Javascript from above with the URL for readinglist.txt from my server:

```
httpGetRiver ("http://fedwiki.andysylvester.com:1337/getoneriver?
fname=readinglist.txt", "idRiverDisplay", function () {
console.log ("startup: httpGetRiver took approx " + secondsSince
(whenstart) + " secs.");
});
}
```

For your setup, replace the URL part (http://fedwiki.andysylvester.com:1337) with the URL for your River5 server, and replace the text following "fname=" (readinglist.txt) with the name of your file in the lists folder within your River5 installation.

Once the editing of the HTML file is complete, you can then upload the file to web hosting provided as part of your account where your WordPress weblog is hosted. Web hosting accounts typically have a folder called "public_html" which serves as a web server for any static content that you want hosted on the Web. The following example will show how to access this folder within the web hosting provided by Bluehost.com.

Log into your Bluehost account, then click on the Advanced menu item in the navigation menu on the left side of the window.

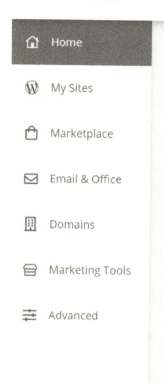

Appendix C - Setting up Rivers of News

The following will appear:

This is the cPanel interface provided by Bluehost, which allows access to all features supported by your account. In the Files section, click on the File Manager link. The following will appear:

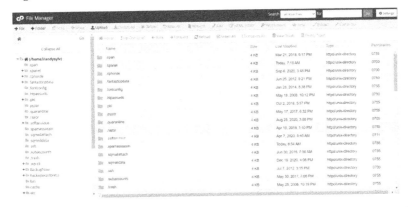

This is a window similar to Windows Explorer on Windows or Finder on the Macintosh. It shows a set of directories that support your web hosting account. In the navigation bar on the left side of the window, scroll down and find the folder called "public_html".

+ 📁 .wp-cli
+ 📁 BackupNow
+ 📁 backupwordpress
📁 bin
📁 cache
+ 📁 etc
📁 ioncube
+ 📁 logs
+ 📁 mail
+ 📁 perl5
+ 📁 public_ftp
+ 📁 public_html
📁 sourceguardian
+ 📁 ssl
+ 📁 tmp

Click on the public_html folder. The following will appear:

The right side of the screen will show a list of all of the folders supporting the website created using your hosting account. It also can be a place to add more content separate from your WordPress website. The next steps in this example will show how to add a folder and upload your HTML file so that it can be seen on the Web.

In the upper left corner of the window, click on the Folder menu in the menu bar. A dialog box will appear:

Enter a folder name in the New Folder Name text box (for example, testriver), then click the "Create New Folder" button. The folder will then be created. If it is not visible, scroll down until you find the folder:

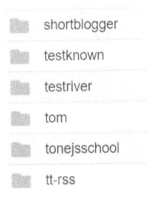

shortblogger

testknown

testriver

tom

tonejsschool

tt-rss

Next, double-click on the testriver folder. The window will update and show the following:

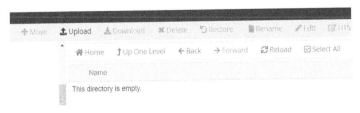

You have a new folder where you can upload your HTML file. To perform the upload, click on the Upload menu in the menu bar. The following will appear:

Click on the "Select File" button. This will open a file dialog window.

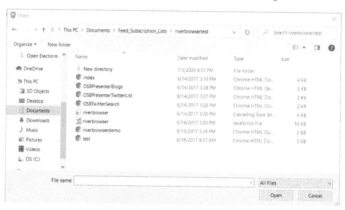

Navigate to the folder where your copy of the riverbrowserdemo.html file is on your computer, then select the file. When the upload is complete, the following will appear:

Now that the file is uploaded, you can look at it on the web. The URL will be a folder based on your primary WordPress site URL. For this

account, the primary site is andysylvester.com, so the URL is
http://andysylvester.com/testriver/riverbrowserdemo.html.

Finally, upload the HTML file to a server. As long as the River5 server is running, your HTML page will display the latest version of the river.

OK – now get started making rivers!

# Appendix D - Getting a Twitter Developer Account

To be able to follow multiple news/information sources, this guide recommends using a feed reader. However, most feed readers are set up to read RSS feeds. A number of social media services (Twitter, Facebook) do not provide RSS feeds any more for users of their services, so how can a user follow these sources separate from the social media service? The good news is there are a number of tools to create RSS feeds for services like Twitter and Facebook, but some of these tools require creating a developer account to access the service using your own tool. This appendix will provide step-by-step instruction for signing up for a Twitter development account. With this account, you can generate access keys that can be used in tools that access Twitter data. Appendix E will demonstrate one of these tools (TweetsToRss) using keys from a Twitter developer account.

## Getting a developer account

To get a Twitter developer account, log into your Twitter account:

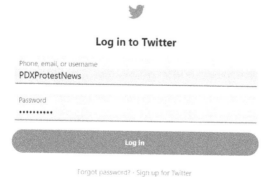

Next, go to the Developer Portal (https://developer.twitter.com/en/docs/developer-portal/overview), then scroll down to the "How to Apply" section and click on the "Apply for a developer account" button. This account will also help you with setup for the TweetsToRSS tool.

The next page (https://developer.twitter.com/en/apply-for-access) has information on Twitter APIs and tools. Click on the "Apply for a developer account" button (links to https://developer.twitter.com/en/apply/user.html):

Get started with Twitter APIs and tools

# Apply for access

All new developers must apply for a developer account to access Twitter APIs. Once approved, you can begin to use our standard APIs and our new premium APIs.

Apply for a developer account    Restricted used cases >

The next page lists options for what you want to do with Twitter developer tools:

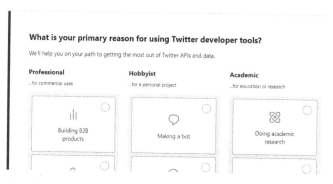

Scroll down in the hobbyist column to the bottom, you will see the following options:

Click on "Exploring the API", then press the Next button in the lower right corner of the page:

The next page will ask for some basic information and confirm that you are applying for an individual developer account.

PDXProtestNews    This @username will be the login for your developer account.

@PDXProtestNews

Switch @username
Create new @username

Individual developer account    You are signing up for an individual developer account. ⓘ

Switch to a team developer account

Fill in the fields, then click the Next button again. The site will then ask you to describe how you plan to use the Twitter API:

**How will you use the Twitter API or Twitter data?**    All fields are required unless marked optional.

**In your words**

In English, please describe how you plan to use Twitter data and/or APIs. The more detailed the response, the easier it is to review and approve.

Response must be at least 200 characters    200

Here is a sample description that fits the the type of tools you will be using:

"I would like to evaluate several tools that can collect tweet timelines for a Twitter user or users via the Twitter API. The tools require the use of keys from a developer account to perform the collection. The information is for my own personal use."

Appendix D - Getting a Twitter Developer Account

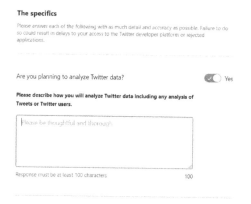

Here is a sample entry:

## Change check box from Yes to No

Here is a sample entry:

## Change check box from Yes to No

Here is a sample entry:

"Tweets will be aggregated by the tools I am planning to use and displayed in a web page. The web page will be viewable on a web hosting service."

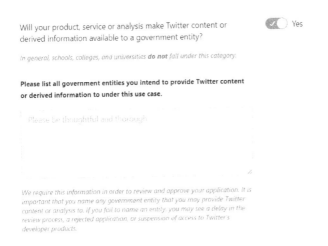

Here is a sample entry:

Change check box from Yes to No

After filling out all forms, click the Next button in the lower right corner of the page. The responses will then be repeated for your review.

If the entries are correct, click on the "Looks good!" button in the lower right corner of the page.

The final step is to accept the Developer Agreement, which is displayed below. Check the box at the bottom of the page and click the "Submit Application" button in the lower right corner of the page.

You will then see a success screen:

You will need to check your email at the address shown on this screen, there should be an email from Twitter asking you to click on a button to verify your developer account. After clicking the button, you will see a web page open with the following:

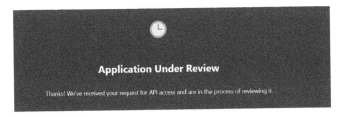

You should also receive another email stating that the application is under review.

Once the developer account has been approved, an email will be sent to the email address associated with the Twitter account. At this point, you can now start to create a Twitter app that will work with server app you will install in Appendix E. To start, sign into your Twitter account, then go to https://developer.twitter.com.

Click on the Developer Portal link in the upper right corner of the page. The Dashboard page will appear.

Select the Project and Apps drop down on the left side of the screen, then select Overview. The following will appear:

Appendix D - Getting a Twitter Developer Account

Scroll down to the Standalone Apps section:

Twitter is moving to version 2 of its API. For now, this guide will focus on version 1.1 of the API. Click on the "Create App" button. The screen will appear as follows:

For this example, enter the name "TweetRSS" as the app name, then click the Complete button. In this case, the response was that this app name was already taken.

# Name your App.

Apps are where you get your **access keys and tokens**, plus set permissions. You can find them within your Projects.

> App name

ⓘ Looks like this App name is already taken. Try a different one.

Back

Try different app names until you can come up with a unique one. After you enter a unique app name and click the "Complete" button, the following will appear:

# Here are your keys & tokens

For security, this will be the last time we'll display these. If something happens, you can always regenerate them.

**API key** ⓘ

**API secret key** ⓘ

**Bearer token** ⓘ

The API key and the API secret key are the two pieces of information that the TweetsToRss tool needs to access Twitter. In the image above, the text has been erased. To easily copy the keys, click on the plus sign at the end of each row. This action will copy that key to the clipboard. Once you have copied a key, paste it into a text file or word processor file, then move on to the next key.

Click on the app name in the left navigation panel (PDXTweetRSS for this example). You should see the following:

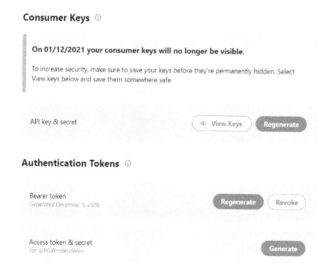

Click on the Keys and Tokens tab, you will see the following:

In the Access token & secret area, click on the Generate button. The following will appear:

Here are your new access token & secret. Have you saved them?

For security, this will be the last time we'll display these. If something happens, you can always regenerate them.

Access token:

Access token secret:

Yes, I saved them

Copy those keys as before. Now that you have created the Twitter app and generated the app keys, you are ready to start using them to enable your server app in Appendix E.

# Appendix E - Running Server Tools That Use Twitter

This appendix will use the access keys generated in Appendix D when the Twitter development account was created. If you have not created a Twitter development account and generated access keys for an app, complete the steps in Appendix D before proceeding with this appendix.

The TweetsToRss tool by Dave Winer is a Node.js app that periodically reads a Twitter account and generates an RSS feed from it. The tool also supports reading a list of Twitter accounts and creating RSS feeds for each of those accounts. The source code and documentation for the tool is available at https://github.com/scripting/tweetsToRss.

## Installation

To get started, log into your Digital Ocean account to access the server created in Appendix A. After logging in and selecting your Droplet, you should be at the Dashboard for your Droplet:

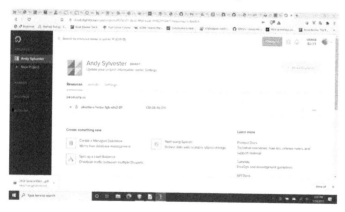

Next, click on the three dots on the right side of the screen of the Droplet box. A set of options will appear in a drop-down menu:

Click on the "Access console" menu item. The following window will appear:

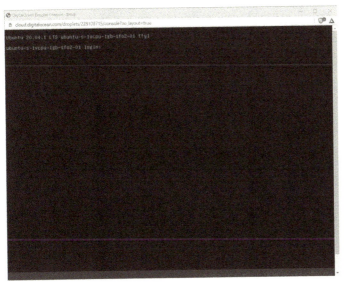

Enter the word "root" without quotes, then press the Enter key. A new line will be displayed asking for a password:

Enter the password that you entered when creating the Droplet. The following will then appear:

If this app is the first app you are installing on your server, use the following instructions from Appendix B to install the necessary tools (node.js, NPM, Git, forever).

In the console, type the following commands in the terminal window to install the following packages:

sudo apt-get install nodejs

sudo apt-get install npm

sudo apt-get install nodejs-legacy (if this command has a problem (see screen capture below), simply proceed.)

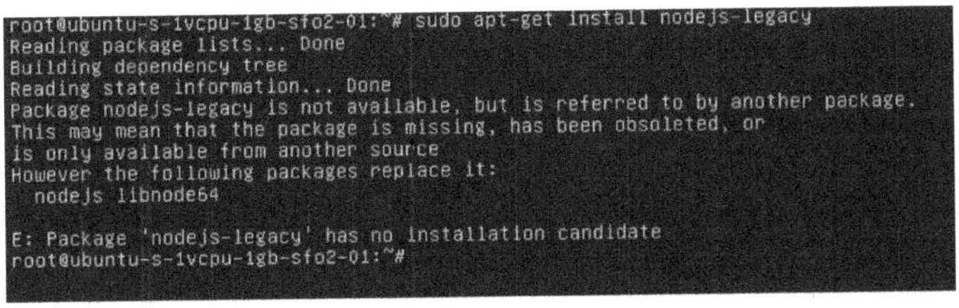

When these commands are entered, the server may list the storage space required for the packages, as shown below:

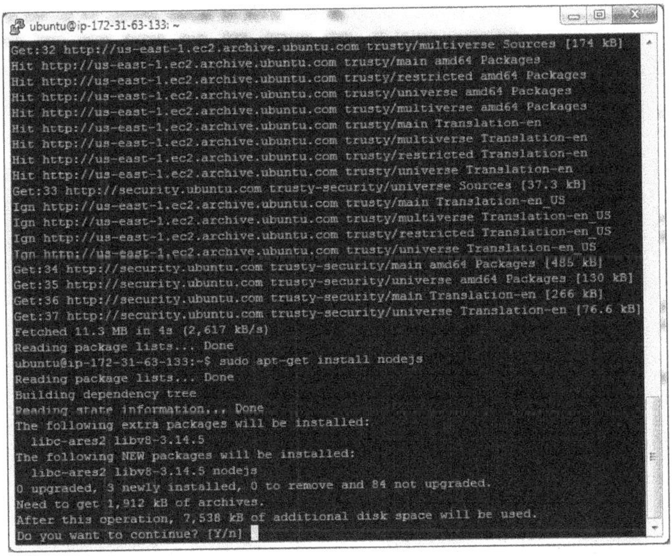

Press Y and then Enter to continue the installation.

Appendix E - Running Server Tools That Use Twitter

After these installations are complete, the Node module called "forever" should be installed using the Node Package Manager (NPM). This will be used later to keep the application running when you are not logged into the server. Enter the following command in the terminal window:

sudo npm install forever -g

Next, the Git configuration management software should be installed. The demo application is stored using the Github service, which uses Git to manage the files. Enter the following command in the terminal window:

sudo apt-get install git (you may get a response that this is already installed, as shown in the screen capture below)

```
root@ubuntu-s-1vcpu-1gb-sfo2-01:~# sudo apt-get install git
Reading package lists... Done
Building dependency tree
Reading state information... Done
git is already the newest version (1:2.25.1-1ubuntu3).
git set to manually installed.
0 upgraded, 0 newly installed, 0 to remove and 72 not upgraded.
root@ubuntu-s-1vcpu-1gb-sfo2-01:~# _
```

To install the tool, type the following command:

git clone https://github.com/scripting/tweetsToRss.git

This command creates a copy of the TweetsToRss tool on the server. Type the following command in the terminal window and press Enter:

ls -l

Note that the command has two lower-case letter L's. This command will list the directory contents. The following text should appear:

```
root@ubuntu-s-1vcpu-1gb-sfo2-01:~# ls -l
total 8
drwxr-xr-x 3 root root 4096 Jan 24 23:20 snap
drwxr-xr-x 3 root root 4096 Feb 21 23:03 tweetsToRss
root@ubuntu-s-1vcpu-1gb-sfo2-01:~# _
```

In the console, enter the following command to change to the tweetsToRss directory:

cd tweetsToRss

Enter the command "ls -l". The following files will be listed as below:

```
root@ubuntu-s-1vcpu-1gb-sfo2-01:~# cd tweetsToRss/
root@ubuntu-s-1vcpu-1gb-sfo2-01:~/tweetsToRss# ls -l
total 40
-rw-r--r-- 1 root root  1078 Feb 21 23:03 LICENSE
-rw-r--r-- 1 root root  2905 Feb 21 23:03 README.md
-rw-r--r-- 1 root root  9622 Feb 21 23:03 exampleFeed.xml
-rw-r--r-- 1 root root   371 Feb 21 23:03 package.json
-rw-r--r-- 1 root root 14730 Feb 21 23:03 tweetstorss.js
root@ubuntu-s-1vcpu-1gb-sfo2-01:~/tweetsToRss# _
```

The file tweetstorss.js is the Node app file. This file needs to be edited to add the Twitter keys generated from Appendix D, when you set up a Twitter development account and generated keys for an application.

The file can be edited on the server or downloaded from the server, edited on your local machine, then uploaded back to the server. For this example, the file will be edited on the server. The Nano text editor will be used for this example.

To start editing, enter the following command:

```
nano tweetstorss.js
```

You should see the following:

```
GNU nano 4.8                    tweetstorss.js
//The MIT License (MIT)

//Copyright (c) 2015 Dave Winer

//Permission is hereby granted, free of charge, to any person obtaining
//of this software and associated documentation files (the "Software"),
//in the Software without restriction, including without limitation the
//to use, copy, modify, merge, publish, distribute, sublicense, and/or
//copies of the Software, and to permit persons to whom the Software is
//furnished to do so, subject to the following conditions:

//The above copyright notice and this permission notice shall be includ
//copies or substantial portions of the Software.

//THE SOFTWARE IS PROVIDED "AS IS", WITHOUT WARRANTY OF ANY KIND, EXPRE
//IMPLIED, INCLUDING BUT NOT LIMITED TO THE WARRANTIES OF MERCHANTABILI
//FITNESS FOR A PARTICULAR PURPOSE AND NONINFRINGEMENT. IN NO EVENT SHA
//AUTHORS OR COPYRIGHT HOLDERS BE LIABLE FOR ANY CLAIM, DAMAGES OR OTHE
//LIABILITY, WHETHER IN AN ACTION OF CONTRACT, TORT OR OTHERWISE, ARISI
//OUT OF OR IN CONNECTION WITH THE SOFTWARE OR THE USE OR OTHER DEALING
//SOFTWARE.
                        [ Read 507 lines ]
^G Get Help   ^O Write Out  ^W Where Is   ^K Cut Text   ^J Justify    ^C Cur Pos
^X Exit       ^R Read File  ^\ Replace    ^U Paste Text ^T To Spell   ^_ Go To Line
```

The cursor keys on your keyboard can be used to scroll up, down, left and right in the file. Also, the copy and paste key combinations (Ctrl-C for

Copy, Ctrl-V for Paste) will also work in the Nano editor. The cursor will be shown as a blinking underline.

Use the down cursor key to get to the following section of the file:

```
var twitterConsumerKey = process.env.twitterConsumerKey;
var twitterConsumerSecret = process.env.twitterConsumerSecret;
var accessToken = process.env.twitterAccessToken;
var accessTokenSecret = process.env.twitterAccessTokenSecret;
var twitterScreenName = process.env.twitterScreenName;
var pathRssFile = process.env.pathRssFile;

var defaultRssFilePath = "rss.xml";
var flSkipReplies = true;

var configStruct = undefined; //1/16/15 by DW
var fnameConfig = "config.json";
```

In the Nano editor, it will look as follows:

The lines starting with twitterConsumerKey through fnameConfig need to be replaced with the following text (where ABCDEF is the text of the keys generated in Appendix D):

```
var twitterConsumerKey = "ABCDEF";
var twitterConsumerSecret = "ABCDEF";
var accessToken = "ABCDEF";
var accessTokenSecret = "ABCDEF";
var twitterScreenName = "davewiner";
var pathRssFile = undefined;

var defaultRssFilePath = "rss.xml";
var flSkipReplies = true;
```

```
var configStruct = undefined; //1/16/15 by DW
var fnameConfig = ""; //"config.json"
```

To edit text in the Nano text editor, move the cursor to the point where you want to start editing, then use the Backspace key to erase, or start entering text. The keys generated in Appendix D match with the variable names as follows:

```
twitterConsumerKey      API Key
twitterConsumerSecret   API Secret Key
accessToken             Access token
accessTokenSecret       Access token secret
```

When you have finished editing, press Control-O to write the file to disk, then Control-X to exit the Nano editor.

Next, enter the following command to install the required Node packages for the TweetsToRss app:

sudo npm install

Text will be scrolling for 10-15 seconds. A new folder (node_modules) will be added to the tweetsToRss folder as follows:

```
root@ubuntu-s-1vcpu-1gb-sfo2-01:~/tweetsToRss# ls -l
total 60
-rw-r--r--  1 root root  1078 Feb 21 23:03 LICENSE
-rw-r--r--  1 root root  2905 Feb 21 23:03 README.md
-rw-r--r--  1 root root  9622 Feb 21 23:03 exampleFeed.xml
drwxr-xr-x 52 root root  4096 Feb 22 00:01 node_modules
-rw-r--r--  1 root root 12848 Feb 22 00:01 package-lock.json
-rw-r--r--  1 root root   364 Feb 22 00:01 package.json
-rw-r--r--  1 root root 14752 Feb 22 00:01 tweetstorss.js
root@ubuntu-s-1vcpu-1gb-sfo2-01:~/tweetsToRss# _
```

Finally, enter this command to start the TweetsToRss app:

node tweetstorss.js

The following text should appear:

# Appendix E - Running Server Tools That Use Twitter

```
root@ubuntu-s-1vcpu-1gb-sfo2-01:~/tweetsToRss# node tweetstorss.js
tweetsToRss v0.45.

everyMinute: 12:03:49 AM
getFeed: 6548 chars in rss.xml
```

This response indicates that a RSS feed for the Twitter username "davewiner" (Dave Winer, the creator of the TweetsToRss tool) has been created in the file rss.xml. Enter Control-C to stop the app.

To see the first part of the file rss.xml, enter the following command:

less rss.xml

The first 20 lines will be shown as below:

```
<?xml version="1.0"?>
<!-- RSS generated by tweetsToRss on Mon, 22 Feb 2021 00:03:49 GMT -->
<rss version="2.0" xmlns:source="http://source.smallpict.com/2014/07/12/theSourc
eNamespace.html">
        <channel>
                <title>davewiner's RSS Feed</title>
                <link>http://twitter.com/davewiner/</link>
                <description>A feed generated from davewiner's tweets by https:/
/github.com/scripting/tweetsToRss</description>
                <pubDate>Sun, 21 Feb 2021 23:57:01 GMT</pubDate>
                <lastBuildDate>Mon, 22 Feb 2021 00:03:49 GMT</lastBuildDate>
                <language>en-us</language>
                <generator>tweetsToRss</generator>
                <docs>http://cyber.law.harvard.edu/rss/rss.html</docs>
                <source:account service="twitter">davewiner</source:account>
                <item>
                        <description>RT @davewiner: Blogging is still with us. h
ttps://t.co/I5Wfvr5wEh</description>
                        <pubDate>Sun, 21 Feb 2021 23:57:01 GMT</pubDate>
                        <link>https://twitter.com/davewiner/status/1363638891673
251842</link>
                        <guid>http://twitter.com/davewiner/status/13636388916732
51842</guid>
                        <source:outline text="RT @davewiner: Blogging is still w
rss.xml
```

The text is structured as an RSS feed. The cursor keys can be used to scroll through the file. To stop, press Control-Z.

This is a good start, but it would be nice if there was a way to have RSS feeds for more than one account, and for the app to run continuously. The following instructions show how to do both of those things.

# Creating multiple RSS feeds

The TweetToRss tool supports generating RSS feeds for multiple accounts using a configuration file called config.json. The tool page on Github has an example file (https://gist.github.com/scripting/2c0c9faacdef884817d7) which is shown below:

```
{
"folder": "feeds/",
"items": [
{
"username": "Circa",
"feedname": "circa.xml"
},
{
"username": "reportedly",
"feedname": "reportedly.xml"
},
{
"username": "davewiner",
"feedname": "dave.xml"
}
]
}
```

This file is structured in Javascript Object Notation (JSON) (more general info available on the format at https://www.json.org/json-en.html). The first item in the file defines the name of a folder where the feeds will be created. In this example, a folder called "feeds" will be created within the folder that the app is running, and the RSS feeds will be stored there. The second item in the file (items) is an array of items containing the Twitter username and a RSS feed file name for each Twitter account to be monitored by TweetsToRss. There is no limit on the number of feeds that can be followed. One thing to note is how the first two objects have a comma (,) after the object closing brace (},), but the last object does not. If you use this file as a starting point, make sure that all objects have a comma present except for the last object in the array. As with the editing done on tweetstorss.js earlier, this file can be created with the Nano text editor on the server, or created with a separate text editor and uploaded to the server. Again, the file name needs to be config.json. To open a new file with the Nano text editor, enter the following command in the console window:

```
nano config.json
```

After the creation of the config.json file is complete, restart the TweetsToRss app using the following command:

Appendix E - Running Server Tools That Use Twitter

```
node tweetstorss.js
```

This time, the app should display a list of file names for the RSS feeds listed in config.json. To check the RSS feeds, enter Control-C after the filenames are displayed, then check the feeds folder to confirm that there is a file for each feed listed in config.json, and that the files have content.

Before running the app continuously, a small change should be made to tweetstorss.js. The default frequency that the feeds are generated is once a minute. This means that the app is calling the Twitter API to get data once a minute for each feed, which could result in a lot of calls if you are following a large number of Twitter users (3600 calls/day x number of Twitter accounts followed). To reduce the number of API calls, change the following line at the end of the file:

FROM:

setInterval (everyMinute, 60000);

TO:

setInterval (everyMinute, 600000);

This will increase the time between API calls from 1 minute to 10 minutes.

To keep TweetsToRss running continuously, another application must be used. The forever Node application was installed earlier in this appendix. Using forever allows a Node.js application to continue running without the terminal window being active. To start TweetsToRss using forever, enter the following command in the tweetstorss directory:

```
forever -o out.log -e err.log start tweetstorss.js
```

This form of the command sends terminal output from TweetsToRss to out.log, and any errors upon ending the forever process to err.log. If you do not wish to collect any information on the application or errors, the command can be shortened as follows:

```
forever start tweetstorss.js
```

Now that these Twitter accounts are being aggregated into a set of RSS files, these could be added to a RSS feed reader app. However, the files are not accessible via the web - the TweetsToRss app only creates the files locally and does not make them available as a web server would. If you have created a WordPress weblog as part of setting up your social media presence, you have web hosting space available that these RSS feeds could be hosted, and then a list of the feeds could be added to River5 or some other RSS reader.

One way to make these feeds available would be to copy them to a web server. Using a script to use File Transfer Protocol (FTP) is one way to do this. Here is an example script:

```
#!/bin/bash

HOST='example.com'
USER='YOUR_USERNAME'
PASSWD='YOUR_PASSWORD'

cd /root/tweetsToRss/feeds
ftp -n -v $HOST << EOT
ascii
user $USER $PASSWD
cd /public_html/tweetfeeds
prompt
mput *.xml
bye
EOT
```

This example script will copy files from the directory where TweetsToRss is storing the RSS feeds to a folder called "tweetfeeds" in the public_html folder on your web hosting account. The 'YOUR_USERNAME' and 'YOUR_PASSWORD' entries should be replaced with the username and password for your web hosting service for FTP access. For some resources on identifying this, see

Appendix E - Running Server Tools That Use Twitter

https://www.bluehost.com/help/article/intro-to-ftp and
https://www.bluehost.com/help/article/ftp-uploading-the-website.

You can use the Nano text editor on the server to create the file (use
instructions given earlier in this appendix) or create it on your local
computer using a text editor, then upload to the server where the
TweetsToRss app is running. To set permissions for executing the script,
enter the following command if the script name is "uploadscripttweets":

chmod 0755 uploadscripttweets

The following will appear in the console:

Reference:
https://bash.cyberciti.biz/guide/Setting_up_permissions_on_a_script

# Scheduling TweetsToRSS

Finally, the cron Linux utility can be used to execute this FTP script on a periodic basis. Cron is a Linux utility for scheduling scripts and commands. There are several options to view current cron jobs scheduled in the crontab list, and to add a cron job (task) to the list.

To list all scheduled cron jobs for the current user, enter the following command:

crontab –l

The system returns an output like the following:

root@AndyDO-03: ~ — □ ×

```
#
# For example, you can run a backup of all your user accounts
# at 5 a.m every week with:
# 0 5 * * 1 tar -zcf /var/backups/home.tgz /home/
#
# For more information see the manual pages of crontab(5) and cron(8)
#
# m h  dom mon dow   command
*/5 * * * * /home/andy/scripts/uploadscriptnew > /home/andy/scripts/backup.log 2
>&1
*/5 * * * * /root/newstest02/feedscript.sh
*/1 * * * * /usr/local/bin/node /root/newstest02/npm run get-feeds && npm run pa
rse-feeds && npm run cleanup && npm run create && npm run search
*/1 * * * * /home/andy/scripts/feedupdate
*/1 * * * * /root/newstest02/feedupdate
*/1 * * * * /root/newstest02/node_modules /root/newstest02/getFeeds01.js
*/1 * * * * cd /root/newstest02 && npm run get-feeds
*/1 * * * * /root/newstest02/node_modules npm run get-feeds
*/5 * * * * cd /root/newstest02 && /usr/local/bin/node getFeeds01.js && /usr/loc
al/bin/node parseFeedsNew01.js && /usr/local/bin/node test02.js && /usr/local/bi
n/node createIndex.js && /usr/local/bin/node searchIndex.js
#*/1 * * * * cd /rootnewstest02 && npm run get-feeds
*/5 * * * * /root/scripts/uploadscripttweets > /root/scripts/backup.log 2>&1
```

Each line in the second screen is a command to run a script at a defined frequency. To add a cron job, enter the following command:

```
sudo crontab -e
```

The following will appear:

```
System load:  0.08             Users logged in:   0
Usage of /:   13.3% of 24.06GB   IPv4 address for eth0: 138.68.45.124
Memory usage: 23%              IPv4 address for eth0: 10.46.0.5
Swap usage:   0%               IPv4 address for eth1: 10.120.0.2
Processes:    90

77 updates can be installed immediately.
0 of these updates are security updates.
To see these additional updates run: apt list --upgradable

*** System restart required ***
Last login: Sun Feb 21 22:47:06 UTC 2021 on tty1
root@ubuntu-s-1vcpu-1gb-sfo2-01:~# crontab -l
no crontab for root
root@ubuntu-s-1vcpu-1gb-sfo2-01:~# sudo crontab -e
no crontab for root - using an empty one

Select an editor.  To change later, run 'select-editor'.
  1. /bin/nano           <---- easiest
  2. /usr/bin/vim.basic
  3. /usr/bin/vim.tiny
  4. /bin/ed

Choose 1-4 [1]:
```

Enter "1" to use the nano editor to edit the crontab file. The nano text editor will open the file as follows:

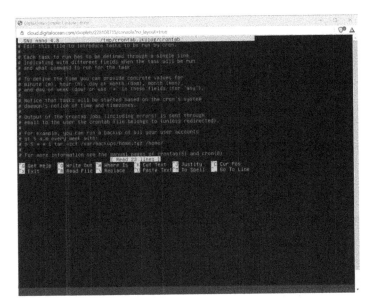

Scroll down to the bottom of the file using the Down cursor key, then enter the following text (including all spaces):

```
*/5 * * * * /root/uploadscripttweets > /root/backup.log 2>&1
```

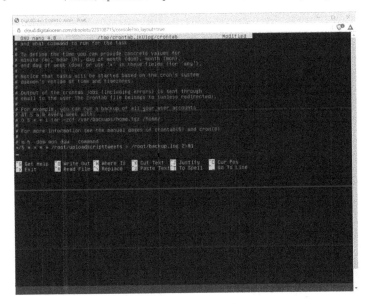

Appendix E - Running Server Tools That Use Twitter

This will add a cron job to call the script uploadscripttweets every five minutes, and copy any response to a file called backup.log.

Enter Control-O to write out the file, then Control-X to exit the Nano editor.

Once the cron job has been running for 20-30 minutes, check on the web hosting server to confirm that the files are being copied correctly. Once the files are there, a new River5 river list can be created to collect the RSS feeds into a single stream.

For this example, create a text file called tweetRiver.txt. Next, add URLs for each of the RSS feeds being copied to the web hosting server. For example:

http://portlandprotestnews.com/tweetfeeds/feed01.xml

http://portlandprotestnews.com/tweetfeeds/feed02.xml

http://portlandprotestnews.com/tweetfeeds/feed03.xml

When the list is complete, copy this file to the lists folder in the River5 install (from Appendix B, this would be /root/river5/lists). After 10-15 minutes, the new river should be available at the URL for the River5 display (from Appendix B, this would be http://134.234.154.64:1337 if your IP address was 134.234.154.64.

If you wanted to have a single page app that could display this river, you could use the instructions in Appendix C to create that page.

Resources:

https://phoenixnap.com/kb/how-to-list-display-view-all-cron-jobs-linux

https://phoenixnap.com/kb/set-up-cron-job-linux

# About the Author

Andy Sylvester has been working in the aerospace industry for over 36 years. He is currently a Principal Software Engineer with Collins Aerospace, and has been a lead software engineer on multiple projects. Andy enjoys creating software, performing music, and writing, not necessarily in that order.

Previous books by Andy Sylvester:

Build Browser Apps Using Google Chrome – Self published book on using the app extension feature in Google Chrome, which has since been removed (sigh!). The online version of the book is available at http://andysylvester.com/buildbrowserapps/.

How to Set Up an A Ubuntu Web Server on Amazon Web Services – Step-by-step guide to creating an account on Amazon Web Service and setting up a server using the Ubuntu operating system. Available at the Kindle Store (https://www.amazon.com/How-Ubuntu-Server-Amazon-Services-ebook/dp/B01HAQ70P4/).

Microblogging: History, Practices, and Tools – An overview of microblogging and its early history, how microblogging is done today, and an overview of multiple microblogging tools. Available at the Kindle Store (https://www.amazon.com/Microblogging-History-Practices-Andy-Sylvester-ebook/dp/B07RDGX6W1/).

To get a PDF copy of this book, forward your receipt to iboughtit@setupyourownplatform.com and a copy will be sent to you!

For more resources or to purchase additional copies, go to https://SetUpYourOwnPlatform.com.

# Index

## Alphabetical Index

www.ingramcontent.com/pod-product-compliance
Lightning Source LLC
Chambersburg PA
CBHW031241050326
40690CB00007B/903